Sueño

Other works by Lorna Dee Cervantes

Emplumada (1981)

American Book Award

From the Cables of Genocide:
Poems on Love and Hunger (1991)

Patterson Poetry Prize
Institute of Latin American Writers Poetry Prize
Latino Literature Award

DRIVE: The First Quartet (2006)

International Latino Book Award
Balcones Poetry Prize

Ciento: 100 100-Word Love Poems (2011)

And numerous chapbooks.

Sueño

New Poems by

Lorna Dee Cervantes

Foreword by Juan Felipe Herrera

WingsPress

San Antonio, Texas
2013

Sueño © 2013 by Wings Press, for Lorna Dee Cervantes

Front cover image: "The Banquet," by Irving Norman (1972)
© 1990 by The Norman Trust.
Collection of the San Jose State University Student Union.
Used by permission.

First Wings Press Edition

Paperback edition ISBN: 978-1-60940-310-2
Ebook editions:
ePub ISBN: 978-1-60940-307-2
Kindle ISBN: 978-1-60940-308-9
Library PDF ISBN: 978-1-60940-309-6

Wings Press
627 E. Guenther
San Antonio, Texas 78210
Phone/fax: (210) 271-7805
On-line catalogue and ordering:www.wingspress.com
All Wings Press titles are distributed to the trade by
Independent Publishers Group
www.ipgbook.com

Library of Congress Cataloging in Publication Data:

Cervantes, Lorna Dee.
  [Poems. Selections]
  Sueño : new poems / by Lorna Dee Cervantes. -- First Wings Press
edition.
     pages ; cm.
  ISBN 978-1-60940-310-2 (pbk. : alk. paper) -- ISBN 978-1-
60940-307-2 (ebook) -- ISBN 978-1-60940-308-9 -- ISBN 978-1-
60940-309-6
  I. Title.
  PS3553.E79S84 2013
  811'.54--dc23
                                        2013005722

Contents

Thirty-Something of the Cruelest

One

Two

Quinto

Foreword

I have known Lorna Dee Cervantes since 1974. Her
poetry has always been razor-beautiful-tender-deep.
Now, in *Sueño*, her work has gathered a unified multi-
voice field and heart-rooted strength. These poems
take flight into unknowable regions—after-lives and
after-deaths and loves and battles. Each line and stanza
carries innumerable visions, soul-music compositions
and image-paints—devouring, alluring, magnetic,
telluric—and dangerous, the way Mayakovsky and
Frida wanted to be dangerous, all acid, devotion and
play. This collection lays out our karma—"our roving
toward God"—the tracks of our indigenous lands, the
moving targets of our national caged rage, our mother-
father-lover yearnings, our woman oceans, and don't
forget, our hipster, tattooed, wounded, still-standing
streets. And there is compassion and homage to Raza
poets that have passed on, Anzaldúa, Arteaga and
Sagel—I miss them and bow here. Lyric rap, healer
woman ripped sonata, Xipe Totec flayed selves—a
"hobby horse of the heart" on fire. This is a lightning
bolt in all its swirling-dissembling appearances. You
have nowhere to run. Lorna says, "I do not enter
lightly," but she does enter with scorching-soothing
light. A total force, a ground-rattling volume—I am
astounded beyond measure. This is one of the bravest,
most timely and duende-diggin' books I have encoun-
tered in decades. I was waiting for this but I didn't
know it until I read it.

—Juan Felipe Herrera
Redlands, California

For my father,
visionary artist, Luis Cervantes,
for the zen

Thirty-Something of the Cruelest

One

"April is the cruelest month."
—T. S. Eliot

First Thought

best thought, you had taught
me — a river runs through it,
the foot of the soul standing
stubbornly in the freeze, all
the shards of ice crumpling up
the banks, what survives
in the ignorance. Play it away.
Be ceremony. Be a lit candle
to what blows you. Outside,
the sun gives a favorite present,
mountain nests in ironic meadows,
otter takes off her shoes, the small
hands of her feet reaching, reaching; still,
far away people are dying. Crisp
one dollar bills fold another life.
You taught me to care in the moment,
carve day into light, or something,
moving in the west that doesn't destroy
us. Look again, in the coming summer,
the cruelest month alive still eats up
the hours. Regret is an uneven hand,
a rough palm at the cheek — tender
and calloused. I drink another glass
of water, turn on the tap
for what grows, for you,
for what lasts, for the last
and the first found thought of you.

The End of the World As We Know It

happens on the dot of an "I", in each
patter of a millipede's feet, in every beat
of a hummingbird's heart. I see the field
frozen to steel, feel the frost split
the single blade, favor the awakening
of a fern frond, feel for the hungry tongue
awaiting the forever ripening. I go out
into the woods, mark my way with a yellow
ribbon, scatter the crumbs of love longing
to get back home. Remembering to close
the door behind me, I breathe in the smell
of my name in the wind, succumb to something
smaller than myself. Feel my way back
to the grinding — my metal
to the pedal, *that awful rowing towards God.*

How to Get A Car Wash

Take a five dollar bill, fold it,
throw it away. Take a penny,
scold it, make it pay and then
spend it. Take a chance, hold it
to your heart, blow on it, send it
to a friend. Take a moment, extol
it, breathe fire into its face.
Face it. Then forget it.

All the ways the highways go,
drive them in a silver sedan.
Ride past the grandmother with the palsied
gait, the old man shuffler by the wooden crate,
the child holding a blue balloon waiting
by the grate. Forget them. Remember
passion. Remember where you put your keys.
Recall registers ringing on Christmas eve.
Record voices and shrill sounds
still ringing in the leaden ear.

Then pay the master, play the slave,
fill up on tanks of rage and rest.
Gun the engines of your folly. Flee
towards the second best, the third eye,
the favored relative, the sullen child
cheered by snow. Feel your way
back to the second crossing. And, there
by the fresh grave in the mirror,
open the hoses, shine the chromey cheeks,
polish the head — and care.

White Walls Are Great For Poetry

Chuy came late or not at all.
He pissed off the principal and pulled
the hair of the pretty chola by the cholla.
He dissed his homework, fed the chinchilla
barbeque Doritos until it died after excreting
a brilliant orange mound of dust. He jabbed
the janitor in the face with his pencil
then furrowed the brow of the brow-beaten
teacher. All the classics passed
him by. All the books with spines
he let fly. He broke the headlights
of the head cheerleader's car then
sling-shot the lights in the parking lot.
He stole all the hotdogs from the cafeteria
then ate all the strawberry popsicles
too. And afterwards, he picked up
a pen, and followed his fate, he
scrambled up to the scribble
letting long vowels and longing
go chomping at the gate, his open
hand, his heart in a great O
of wonder. *Oh, white walls are great
for poetry.*

Friendly Fire

He was the friendliest fire
you'll ever meet, the burning brow,
hawk-like — eagle-eyed and splendid,
black wings opening when he looked at you;
you, stunning in the view. He had a vein
constricted at the temple, a single throb
pulse of rage before he hit you.

The most beautiful man you'll ever meet,
full of *I love yous* and honey, the stick
and sweet spoil of summer sweating off
that brow. He'll need you. He'll time you,
ride you 'til it hurts. Be a word
he doesn't speak, a turn of phrase
in French, something foreign to this land,
the red dirt that birthed him — first son
of a lost civilized tribe. He was the most
too good to be true you'd ever seen
and then you vanished

under a lump on your head the size
of an apricot, plum-colored, plush.
Just you, first. First Nation
penalty. He was the friendliest
fire you had ever smoked. He was
the quickest burn in an underground forest
of men. He was the timber, a tender fire,
and going down in flames.

Our Ways, Our Whys

Why does the season fly off
the handle? Why do the trees
resist the birds, the passive
passing of autumn, the migratory
monarchs? Why does the single
stand of oak still long
for the acorn? Why does the milk
sour and lie?

Our ways wind across the valley
of our lost loves, the beaten paths
pour into rivers of rain. The ways
of children hurt us, often. The why
of willful folly, the why of sinful
golly still hovering over pursed lips.

Why does the winter hold us
to the fire and then let go?
You hold a hand, forgetting to let go
of the heart. You see a flower
still holding to the petal and
blow it off. Your fingers, a ring
of fate — then, take it off.

The Milk That Does Not Lie

Between fever and fewer
she lay there, faceless
and defaced, she lay there
expressing less, needing more
than a handle to hold her,
wanting more than a crank to
start her, a locked chest,
a box of hope or sorrow's key:
the latch that would unhook her.

He held his own, the vanished skyline
over the ridge of memory. Her hair
brushing the softness from his face
as he looked at her, unseeing.
Defacing as she lay there. Heaven,
a fatal flaw, a missed exit,
a feeling.

Ornery

'Twas an ornery wind
blew in that summer sadness,
that twisted the trees and the lumps
in the hearts — all those hearts thumping
that day, that train-blasted winded
day the levee didn't hold. *Hold on!*
was the rains' echo, and its past,
the summary of scattered pages,
jackets sog-strewn and bogged down
in the comprehension of it. Incomprehensible.
All etched into history: the upside
down non-survivors strung up on the crossing.

You look out there, that sad somewhere
cresting, that homesake sinking
it in. *I'm beginning again*, and truth
is all they have to say, the trailer
bound, high-mark lifted souls in shatters,
these shackles of survival hanging on
a phone call, FEMA, the men in charge
while memories mold and families hunger
and the old just can't take any more.

Will you take this loaf of bread?
Would you trade this big screen
for a loaf of time? Would you shoot it
in the air for them to come to you, give water
to the baby who does not cry again?
Just to say — *I'm here. Come out and save me.*

Sweet Sugar On Brown Dresses

Memphis Minnie stole the show
twangin' and wailing on her electric guitar,
making the trains sing through the blood of the dancers,
their sewing machines stitching brown uniforms into souls
through their steps, the dance taking the hand of sorrow
for a spin. She would plan the great escape, Sojourner
searchin' for her truth — all gussied up and settling
for a six-string happiness. *Next train to Clarksville.*
It's a long walk home. I been there: taxi ride crosstown
with the Pakistani driver who was born there. "Sure,"
he said, "Chicago paper just ran a big spread." Her stance,
her grinning gold, the accents of her indigenous brows
even near death, a face and the paralyzed hands folded
on the porch in Memphis. Another photograph. Another kind
of home, far from the stockyards, the killing pens, the Sundown
Laws. It was not that "my man done left me," that pleading
through the night, it was that "I hate to see that evening sun
go down" when The Law had the right to arrest you, you,
an "unaccompanied Negress," rape you, beat you, sterilize you,
and abort your child *when the sun go down....*

Night Travelers

In the icy dawn, black fascism rides,
the black boot to the dream, the handcuff
to the groin, the indigenous gate
locked shut to the immigrant fate.
Every eyeway sees: the mirrored shades,
the ominous way power's slender wire remains.
This is my country, a country between us, a hard
wired pride in history, in the way we were, and will
be — ever free, the ability to stop this: the burning
van, the raping man, an icy waiting child in Greeley.

Blind Desert Snakes

Across the immigrant road, wisps of ice
knot and unknot sinews of light and water,
water the parched mouths crave. The voiceless
snakes of a voiceless race wage across the desert
landscapes. An empty field waits for the wake.
Blind desert snakes, the sinuous ghosts of the ones
gone down unreel: the young man left behind, the wan
girl taken and raped. The scratched out eyes of freedom
shrivel at the weight. Dignity's dried arroyos
wait for the spring of our change. Give it. *¡Justicia!*

Wet Feet

You married a wetback,
my mother would say. Remembering that
startles the migrant starlings into battle
against the annihilation of autumns past.

In a hurricane season they come, hands
that know how to pick up sticks, legs
that remember the walk. Perhaps empathy
has played out her part. Maybe the vast breadbasket
of summer revved the tornado over Wichita's heart.

What we remember remembers us, these threats
of delay and departure, that stalling at the altar, that settling
at the table of despair. Where is the medicine
for the condition of injustice? What line
do I sign the treaty that gets you off —

the boot at the neck, the hand on the pistol,
the wretched signature of discovery
and compiling interest? I take this
as I am: a country of error,
a willing sacrifice, repair.

Kitchen Grief

See the buzzards over Boulder
today. Dead hot. Earthquake weather
if it'd been on the coast. Circling
calculation. What station the next
body lay? The birds bunch above the quad
over the head of an upturned Dalton.
Trumbo's all handed, all heart mission.
The bay of sky opening to the merchant ships,
the clouds, the few skiffs of passion
still lingering around the campus. Jesse,
dead but not yet buried, laid out today,
his boyish laugh laid to rest — un sueño
in a glass of remembrance. The promise
of spring heavy as the odor of a hung-over
senior. All the misconceptions loaded
in a carafe of courage. These bold plans
now a kitchen of grief, the feasting
yet to come. And a single contract
is signed with a pledge of loyalty
and a drink to that. As the buzzards
of Boulder move up for a closer inspection
in this season of suicide and falling grades,
a full-blown something laid to nest
beside the roadside — a ring of caps,
a circle of camps.

Moonlight In Vermont

lit up the fire of rebellion,
you, in your woody wagon
that hadn't been washed since 1972.
"This car runs on alcohol, drugs and
guns" a fingerprint in the grime declared at the border.

Someone's published fate hung in the error
and the going on — despite. In spite of the crime
you hunkered down downtown, hungry and angry
at the "Reich Likes Ike" button on the wall of your past,
the latenight telephone calls to the dead dad
who routinely tied you down to a red desk until you
got the grammar right, the argument
that came to blows between a son and his
father — there in that paper stack room,
that chamber of the heart's interrogation — the placement
of the period, in or out of the brackets
of a saying, telling, that multiple embrace of the notice.

I notice this particular season, same light
of a particular night in Vermont, passing through
with you and your "illegal alien" bride
going home to a place you'd never been,
never seen, among the placid cows I dread;
still inside a pen and the razor of the keys
and truth on that old Olympia, the constant pecking
order, the link and chain. The drive.

Testimony, Trial

So many damaged souls,
the many souls of the Maya
now reduced to one mumbling
into eternity past. The simple
street scene, the reek. No one
to wash. No one to watch.
The many, stupefied into spectacle
on a San Francisco street — far from love.
Alone, together, they gather on the corner,
line the center: wild ivy on a sideways tower.
Escaped from themselves, they lie
against the hardened offices, guttered
and guttural against the elements
of an elemental losing. Touch them.
Give them a cent. Re-center them
with sleep. The stark reruns unwind
indefinitely. Stalling. Stalling
at the testimonial chalice — a witness,
a leathered bound book, a trial:
this person. *Here.*

Sandwiches

Fortune tells its spread,
the lay of the hand, the second
check, the clear smear of future
cast in fate. I pretend to care,
to share my rare and tenuous thread,
the shred of substance in the guessing.

All I know is a certain air, an invisible
longing towards the flame of flare, how
everything crumbles past the touch. I feel
my way, the web of possibility. The last
step, secure in the knowing I don't know.
All in there, that hollow of alone — is shared.

The crisp husk of morning leaves
off her battle, the new won day
brilliant with bursting through. I rule
another mile of minutes, these shoes.
I choose another opening to be
sandwiched in — all resonance and light.

Candy Bar

Every night he ate a candy bar,
a peanut butter hope, the muscular
spread in the middle, the acid sweet
nougat. He ate for the aid
of something larger than himself,
that filling to fill, that fullness
in the heart that never comes. All the repetition,
the attention to latinate names for
the flexing, all those stubborn glutes and glut
and max', all the careful measuring of aminos,
the building blocks of a new tomorrow
in a new physique — anything to lay
it on. Every night, that wrinkling of the wrapper,
a calling to God to come on over and get him.
He was getting larger and no longer
the stiff face in a morning mirror. Every night
that gnawing into shame, that fighting
with the self for the room to move,
for the single soul, full-grown, with a view.

The Best Seven Minutes of My Life

were spent with you. How many poems
open like that? How many yous open like that
to a touch? Your delicate face in my palms,
the blush of our truth on your cheeks. What sudden
love, yes, struck silly talking, a new you pressed
to my hips. We were a way out of that cul-de-sac
of our fin d' siècle. We were a single wave
pushing into a shore — our lives, unfolding
before us: all the chip-lipped cups and the books,
the rats stacked up in cages, your instruments
and their cases completing the high-rise cityscape
in the kitchen. How I cooked for you, love
in the making, our love-making made permanent
in the stamping. Yes, I loved you. Yes, you were
the love of my life — that time. Yes, we were.
Though we never made that summit and made love
in a tent above treeline. I never stopped wanting
you. You, in all your delicate shards and ways,
curling to me, covering me with your boney
wires, all the you coming out of you,
all the ways to live and love in seven
minutes of wonder, and wounding, or less.

The Oranges At the End of the Meal

There were oranges at the end of the meal
and oranges at the start in the salad, and
an orange peel of your long ponytail satiated
and served. Your sweet lips still pursed
to the tartness in that garden. Nothing sweet
could end that fantasy meal. The poached mandarins
puzzling the bloody meat all night; and when it hit
the flames and the succulent dying began again
in the dying dusk, we licked the beasts we were.
All night awake for you. All day, the pungent night
remembering in the whiff of your scent. All animals
came to the remembering fire, a ring of fire
like in Cash's wife's remembering hit song
as I watched the wood flare into working coals.
All that work that hid you away from our
particular sorrow. All the ways I made you
wait.

How Good Sleep Sounds

to the unimpaired. Those little tics
that punctuate the day, those minor faces
of despair wearing away the cement
of our care. The sound of breakers
in one stomach. The tuba of nightmares
blaring through the chorus. The fine aria
of children spinning away into meadows
of bones, the spattered remains of their
fields. A parent's midnight striking
the finite hours, hoping for a dream,
the miracle mile of the sudden rested.
How good sleep sounds, the waves of nostalgia
rocking the most distant heart. Have
a pillow. Halve it into pleasure and pain,
the dual mask of the dead. All voices
now coming into shadow. A part of the giant
mystery, the sexual coming —
                              I remember you
how you loved in that moment, glad-hearted
to be bedded, the sleep in your sip,
the wine in your eyes, that glossy effect,
the post of your arms around me. How good
that sleep now sounds.

Tension In the Body

You wore it well, that swell,
that leaden grin you practiced.
Your ballerina grace now gracing
the table of your disgrace. What you
chose to hide now thumping at the gate
Like a grand balloon emerging too soon,
its clumsy float beyond your reach,
beyond you, stuffing it into your pillow,
putting it back into that empty trunk
of desire, that restless opening.
Why do we survive? This tension
in the body falls apart at the slightest touch.
Some languor at the wayside of the muck,
a fine depression now lining your pewter face.
The mask of your continence, the flare
of your manicured hair, all the ways
you were suppressing it — all the whys
we'll never know; How, now, will we
ever know?

Heart-Shaped Scars

All around, the heart shaped scars,
the hidden claws surrounding. She looks out
upon a sea of high wounds, the shotgun shells
clattering at her feet. A world around her
and all she thought to call was the wooden police
who would not come, or when they did they smirked
into the midnight of her stark heart so
used to the abuse. The minute wings
of new flies joined in the cacaphony of chaos,
hard flecks of left still clung to the chipped plates,
a sucking sound harbored the toilet, all the
disrememberings left to overflow in the waste.
She and I, an anomaly, Ten Little Indians
and then us, last. We wove our way out of the maze,
the race behind us now sweating at the gate.
All the ways we played, the shadows on the wall
telling us our future, fortune formed by a play of hands,
the thumb out you show — or no. All around her,
the shadow play: a Punch and Judy massacre,
all bloodless and wit. The heart shaped scars
of a silent war that punctuate her living, undeclared
in the waiting from birth. Her, her little soldier, all
uniformed and bright.

In And Out

for Mom

How you wanted release
from the rusted cage. Those frayed
bolts that cut your wrist, the scar
above your heart I suckled to,
that red opening sealed inside your clothes.

How you bit at the bit, gnawed
at the knobby cells surrounding you,
all those metal shards between your
teeth, biting still through my childhood
dreaming. How I never wanted to be you.

In and out and in and out goes the wooden
saw, the hobby horse of the heart
you rode through a blazing hell. You pull
me by the hair, by my dream
braids from the hearses with your
heedless housemaid's hands.

Honoring Past, Present, Future

I woke to a dream of wild horses
but they were there, just woken up
on the plain. Their burr-ridden manes,
brushless and matted, the sensitive muzzles
nuzzling their loves. The bolt-upright colts
charging the wire of the fence that separates
the class from phyla, the elegant four-leggeds
from the two-footed beasts. The unshod shone
there, the black stallions and the paints, long
past their Indian riders or the metallic helmets
and spurs, long past the whip and the spit
of the bit, ridden past the memory of horses
going into the gate, the hobbled run, the unsteady
gait no longer a reason to die. I could have tied
one to this train, or lassoed a mare
or snapped a picture of that remembered
friskiness in the autumn. I could have
drawn them, the sensitive eyes. I could
have honored them, there, the wealth
of a nation stamping over gopher holes.
I could have given them my apple,
my free reins, my heart. My past,
present and future, just a bare-backed
dream of passing, the hidden saddle,
the forgotten lure of history.

Stenciled Memories

for Gra'ma

There was always fabric in your lap
and a whistle in your heart. A sweet
sap to be sucked waited in the garden.
Nymphs of newts nestled under rock,
your role as *She Who Brings the Waters*
intact. Between the trilling of the crickets
educating into the night and the sad sack
of cans in the mornings something grew,
flourished in the dark — vines as sturdy
as telephone wire writhed in the breezes.
You patched together a blanket of us,
sewed together the mismatched and lopped
off edges. And anger grew a twin, ripped
through the bermuda grass, something stubborn
and determined: Me, in a leather patchwork skirt,
the bitter lemon song returning to its beginning
over and over on the Howdie Doody phonograph,
a handful of bandages, a faceful of ghosts
delivered from the mirrors. How did you stand it?
All of it. Us crunching through your set life,
kids scuffling through the mounds of leave.
Always making do. Your sunshine eyes,
those stenciled memories where
we still live.

Her Shallow Grave

was sudden, was a forest of change,
not even a breathing apparatus in sight;
all the moon-struck streets emptied of Halloween,
a shroud of decency suspended in the wake.

Hers was a sudden sorrow. I walked
holes in my shoes, neglecting the birds, the
could-have-been-hers. All the wicked ways
summer can catch up with you again.

Remember the rain, heart. Be well
for winter.

Thirty-Something of the Cruelest

Two

"A poetic image is the soul
inaugurating a form."

—Gaston Bachelard

Language

Grandma told a story of want and can't.
There was never such a word she insisted.
So when I pointed to her twisted spine
and the coin on the floor, she slapped me.
"Where there's a will there's a way," I say
to remind me. And think of you, asleep
in your heart, that house of cards.
The silence of worms fasting and fusing,
the crime of their slime, brilliant
and fulfilling: the order of their days,
their ambiguous mating — all seems
a syntax of sense and decision. In the final
episode of you you're a bad cliche
I can't resist. You're the other shoe
falling, the last note of Taps. You're
the bugle to the fox and I am exhausting.
You're the story I never found the end
to write. You're the last act and all the understudies,
sick. I think of you when I want to close
my purse, the parched lips, the fast
hands. Grandma held us in a tale of want
and I-can't-let-go. I can't let him
become you, or the shatter — the will
that just can't find its way.

Silver

for Dad

suddenly appears the day after you went,
after spring pretended to die and the left
behind clouds decided to snow; the blizzard
happened in the midst of your constant laugh,
my last remembrance of you. Every time you are here
you are laughing — that host, the mind's eye, grinning.
Now the mountains have lost their silver threads,
the hot rock reddens with the sun, and I think of you,
the gray hairs you teased me about wanting. "Stick around,"
you said, "you'll get them." The western landscape punctuates
the sky, the lost score of the peaks waiting to be sung.
I wish away the life I was without you, the handy
threads I pull to get away, the reasons,
unreasonable then, for why you left. And now,
without you, I feel your hand on my shoulder,
the steel of your fingers guiding, and the Light —
the light there — right there, providing.

Love

What I need is a guy
with grace, with a face
only a tortoise could love.
Could you fill it? this whole
gasp scape of cunning? this avalanche
of famish and feast? I leaven the bread
and knead longer to expose the self.
This chaff and fly, this getting by,
this sure slide to you: this match
and tie, this net leap: shake and weave.

Yes

I could hold you on the way down.
This tree called my spine and its delicate
lace of leaves, the heaving shudders
in the shadows, the divine inspiration
of these cords and chording, will stay.
I'll fret the stops, bear down on the way
into you. Inside me (the summer, the sudden
palacio de fuego, fierro del mar, cobre),
the fine feathers of an ancestral hush — over me,
you, orange, an infinite first peel, reeling.

Allure

Autumn's a lure
of anything goes — let fly
your seed pods, left behind
lovers; ubiquitous paper
colored to season decorates
the halls of dailiness. This down
here thinks it is a hurricane
going down. Baja inscribes the bay
with fast food wrappers, hypodermic
discards and the dregs of hangovers.
Over substance: the fine sheen
of flesh, the market of memory
hankering for a sell. Will you be
that video, playing all day in the hot
house of a dream? Could you shed
the particles of what you were — that
mood in the grass, that turning? I let go
and glide into my future as the rest
of this tree, this heartwood, here,
foreign and carved into the symbols
of something I'm wrought. Will you go
with me to market? Can you share this shed,
mill in the departments of the loveless?
Lured into meadows and small mountains
of leaves — these beginnings, those left.

Slaughterhouse

slide — all the way to the
grave, a grading off the mount.
The sideshows of summer settle
the score. The carnies call and cull
the crowd for a willing mark. Three
tries for a dollar, and a whimper
for your rent. The lithesome treaties
walk away; the wild get wilder, all
it takes is a little show. You up
the ante. Call it a draw. While
your life chugs along at a particular
stew. Can you stir the pot forever?
Somewhere cattle are shifting, the plains
settle into snow. Your everywhere
is sudden and surrounding, the smell
of you — and fear — some kind of substance
penetrates. Waiting with the tractor,
the boards in place, the bars, the hinges,
I'd follow you anywhere. It's the story
of attraction. Now, a chute for a life,
this final squeeze into the pen.

Polygamy

They practiced in the west
and by Moslem women refused.
And the Great White Way
proliferated across the plains
in the furrows of one man
and a woman's willing air. Who claims
this heir? Of woman born and named
by no man — that no man's way
of being invisible in this land. Here,
the broad hips of the breadbasket
girdle around envy. The starved eyes
of silent America play on the jukebox.
Everything empties down the sinks in Little America.
Here in the middle everything grows, whole
forests of change wait your burn.
Would you give it a match?
To get by? Over the edge I prefer
the wedge of the poverty I skirt. Here, am I,
contiguous at last.

Hometown

Hometown
pride, side
of beef hash

way
of mash
and mashed. Fried

elegance
throughout, safe
in shade. Shady

days
ahead. Led
out of water.

Oxygen

You were an in way out, full-blown
panic in a parka. The angels
wrestled into substance in the snow
lay for us, expressing. Laid out
between the pee rings, the ghosts of us
loved eternally into the reasons, seasoned
errors, arreared into another penalty
before payday; they lay there, looking at us.
We, burning, believing into another century,
melt into the mold. We select furniture
and argue. We put up sconces, ensconced
in our own individual dreams of tomorrow.
Will this fit here? This heat, this heart, this sacrifice?
I put you here — where I'll forget. The photo
of us in relief, the military armor of a jaded
adolescence holding us right. Would you
remember me, the way I fashioned myself
then — a bright balloon of down, a punctured
raft of sleep, a tied down stay, a phantom
breath of our last mingled, bungled kiss?

Hunger

Hunger heals the hardened heart
in an ideal world. The hunger of mares
filling up the field. The hunger of rare
fish kissing every bit they see, the wild
hunger of those who fly and dive, a hunger
of the hole and the whole world giving
up. The hunger of a racing mouth, the hunger
of parchment for the pen, a hunger of
music to the violin ... hunger redeems
her book of blank food stamps, holds
the hot pot to the breath. Hunger stamps
around and displays in the kitchen. Whomever
marries hunger growls into traffic
at the forced stop, lunges at hunger
as the knives play out. Sing to hunger
in order to appease her. Or, hunger
heals the wound it opens. hunger quenches
the thirst of whales. Hunger opens her
eyes in the kiss, her hair falling down
masking your eyes. Hunger flies
out fast and all alone, back to the
reunion. Hunger, who's fast on her feet,
hunger who can't stand still for the fast.

Ver

for Gloria Anzaldúa

When you're copper poor, all
you have left is the walk.
The get up and go got you
there, and you stuck in the craw,
devoid and raw, an envelope at your
feet, taped shut. You did anything
to open it. You challenged. You braided.
You swung wide the gate. The goal was not
an absence — it was demanding the presence.
Demanding the sea. Upbraiding. See?

Homegrown

Homegrown girls in the Mission
sprout and seed under a chola sun,
the coming back after never having left
still fresh on their breath, the morning pain,
the evening dulce, the wicked mambo
of their hips. On their lips, silence and song,
sweet sambas of eyelashes sway and see:
the morning traffic, the evening crowd;
a certificate of belonging painted by their voices.
All around, the odors of food and decay,
what's made and left. A scattering of pigeons
in their steps. Black clouds of gum
on the pavement. Red pools of blood.

Movement

There was always someone trying
to stop us, shoot out our lights, cover
our mouths with their laws and trials.
It was about breaking through and breaking
out. The bars and the glass, the coded wars
and the brass, the crass class lines we
dared not cross. *Jesus Saves* hanging over us,
the sign, a miracle heading straight to the grave.
Colored butterflies, pin-struck and perishing, we flexed
our wings and, winging it, we fled. We led. We fed.

Tiny

Tiny watched out the side
of her mouth, talked out
of turn. Her sinuous sorrow
tied up in a bundle of charm.
Her tattooed arms, a guest register
in ink — the ball-penned manner, the eloquent
script, the medieval illuminations pinned in pink.
She never left off or ever let it go: the barrio bulldog,
a so-and-so. She taped her bangs into letters, formed
us, troops. She's still there — 15 years of nesting
pleasure — RIPped.

Puppets

Somebody gave her a hand,
put themselves into her: a skirt
filled out, a blouse blossomed.

Somebody opened her voice box
and wound her ardor. Somebody stroked
her as he stoked her, made her stand up.

Somebody picked out her words
and put them in her small corners,
her secret patches, her hidden vestibule.

Somebody took up the strings
of her falling down, propped her up
beside him and removed the stuffing.

Somebody played her at their stage,
supplied the plot and props, made her
the fall guy, the butt of the joke.

Somebody picked her off the shelf,
she thought, had saved her sand
for the best and last, had restrung her:

His puppet, His entire show.

Resurrection

Come and dig out the worms of deception,
pull the fist of history out from the mouths of babes.
Red earth buries the dreams of the old ones.
The young refuse. The dead talk back. Listen.
Weighted fields whither under the hoary frost.
What bulges under the beaten ground? What hands
stay trampled under? Fingers of saplings
stroke the sudden blooming. A new light
flickers in the leaving. On and on, the rising:
the poor, the dejected, the rejected rise. Anew.

Burial

Under the burning stones, between the skins
of mudflats and the clay tablets of a trash abandoned
river I see you: mounds of the living under the flesh
of the dead. Piquant wafts of your shreds, the ragged
flags, a putrid longing to belong, to sing once again
a hallowed song of self in a place. Under the open freeway
lanes, a voice in the rush of rush, a bare tunnel
asking the question: *What is buried here? Who thrusts
out among the living chalk?* Who answers an unasked
question: *All of America is an Indian burial mound.
Anew.*

Indigena

There are some who braid and some
who unravel. There are some who shave
and some who blossom into moss and
string. There are some who are brave
and some who run across tomorrow.
There are some who lie awake listening
and some who waken with a bell.
There are some who pry apart billfolds
and some who reel in the fish. There are
some who rely on the few doors of the seasons
and some who live by colored calendars and pens.
There are some for whom starlight
is a beacon for travel, and others
who want to lock it away. Summer chose
the old ones. Today we, we could save
a way of life and pay — dollars for difference.

Permanence

Think, *rock*. Say, *scissors*. Be paper
in a safe. The river rides a far away rapid.
Nothing to do with you, it sings to say.
I wander the banks, empty the funds of tomorrow
in the time it takes to cup my hands. *Here is my river,*
and aspen leaves fill in the hollows. *Here is my sun,*
and a gold stream of leavings shatters the hold
of the wind. Let me count it to the grave. Let me sing
of love's showers, the hours until I open the maw
of the blades, hear the crinkle of heart, the hammer.

Semi-Square

He was half out of the box,
a lanky leg and head sticking out.
He was all crammed in together
with the lost ghosts of past
loves and long avenues of desire.
He was stuck in the hope
of freedom: to live free
in another's eyes, to love
without walking away, without locking
the world out of his heart.
He was semi-square, a taut
angle, an acute but lone corner.
He gifted the key to others
who went away with that jangling
in their pockets. He wanted to be
loose in the atmosphere, a cosmonaut
in solo flight, the discoverer
of his own New World.

Thunderheads

for Jim Sagel, a Chicano poet

Here in the landscape of you
everything happens, every day the feathering,
the new beginnings, the endings.
You chose to end it, to go back to the land
and pray with the noose and your bowed neck,
the black belt that held everything in
until then. The bulky mass above the Sandía
mountains doesn't tell, nor do the birds
with their social chatter. The mysteries of wind
whisper through the gaps in the living mortar,
but don't recite the litanía of your pain,
the ring on your finger you were about to remove,
the divorce of place as much as the parting
of ways — all that you couldn't say
to no one. Now, thunderheads pick up the call,
a healing rain, a puddling of getting by.
You're moving past us, a blue fog,
an odor of piñon — a line we read
which comes back to us in the sorrow
of morning, the bare wisps of memory
decoloring the blue above Socorro.

Promise

Flute tulips before the storm, the ease
of snow over the hail. Come and freeze me
to a crisp of silence. Let me look at you
until the light flickers and the empty bowl
of the world gone you expires. Let me handle
this flame, the flare ahead that becomes you,
your hands, the softest nest of hair. Find me in
a brittle state, the window of your glow, warming, in
the sit-down say-it of cardinals, weaving, the busy blue
birds rendering happiness into silken sheaves the length of you.

Strength

All I ever had was strength.
I show it in the cracks. I smooth
out stone on stone, I sheen with use.

All I've ever known was shame
and philosophy: *Plato's Republic,*
The Birth of Tragedy, Young Werther's Sorrows...

I have an affinity with the sea,
my sailor's blood, my stance:
my wild stallion, the waves

I do not enter lightly. I moan
and creak, the leather of a slave.
I can take the heat; hell, a sudden parting.

I do not know. I hold
fast, the spirit text: the great
death inside us; strong, inside us.

Radiation

Words can stop a meltdown.
Splinters of where we live can heal
a fissure. The expansion
of a sudden mystery, the heart
stunned into being. Words of another
nation, under bark, transformed.

The tree holds, ever after.

Integrity

Yours is the integrity of flint,
of steel, of iron. Yours
is the integrity of birds flocking,
whales in their loving pods. Yours
is the integrity of sand, what moves
with the will of you; all your sweet
sweat, your simple construction.
I love the sudden fill of you, your
swell and sway. I love how you do
what you say. You slay me
with your truth. I love the way
we fit together as if I were your
seed. I love the far away look
in your multicolored eyes, the land
and sea of you. I love
the way you look at me, that ancient
shore. I love how I am more
with you, your carbon, the filaments
of your fine hair. I love how you hold
me together, how fast and vast
the ocean of this love in its gentle
tide, the integrity of flesh, of salt,
of we.

A Bit of Grace

Trey

In order to dance
In order to dance La Bamba
One needs a bit of grace
A bit of grace
—Trad. Mexican song

Burn Ward

I would love you like Walt
Whitman loved his fellow man,
like a volunteer in the Civil War loves his wards.
I would pack up your abscesses,
pile on the cotton 'til what bleeds
ceases and you cease to amaze you.

I would love you like Walt Whitman
loved the turtles, the small places
in a body a soul can hide.
I would love you like skin loves
the taste of salt, like water loves
the high mark. I would love you,

love the keloids of your flesh
hardened into hands, love
the damp epitaphs, the masking sensuous lines
of your forehead — no matter the pain.
I would dip my cloth into your opening.

I would leave it there, some new marble
of me grafted to your hide.
I would sacrifice my ice and tears,
my bandage of lip and mouth, my art
of putting back the you that falls apart.

People Talking In Their Sleep

Who comes out of that dead end
alive, untouched? The surface
of glass, gasping with breath,
the thick gauze touched up
with sighs. Out of the woodwork
of dreaming comes freedom
from the dance of life, comes
the future in a wheel-barrel
filled with the nickels of nightmare.
Come up on the stoop, play
the marbles in your head
through the gritting teeth.

All the truths of summer
slumber there on a dime.
All the wits of winter
wake up to grumble of game.
All the leavings of autumn
cry out through the teeth
of sleep — in the dream
talking to its person.

Doppelgänger

Stare into the ice chest of autumn, past
the lake and out into the river of years. Believe
the self reflected there, the shadow.
Put your hand into its mouth, and pull,
the doppelgänger of all you left
behind returns. That man buying a newspaper,
the deaths folded into a fan of stain, the pages
that become you in the end. The woman
buying chicken, the flower of her blossoming
into another. The child with his wooden
ball. The girl with her strident monkey.
Mirrors surround us, unseen or not.
Ready or not, they are meeting in the subway.
They are locating the lost relatives.
They are you. Or not.

Stress and Distress

It was just the stress, he tells me.
All that he didn't do, the demands on his
time, the unfinished rhyme of his love.
It was the distress of a broken hip,
the bone that pierces down to home.
The window to a dream painted shut,
the 24/7 of making a killing. It was just
the timing, the hour, the play-it-again waiting.
It was illness in the packing, a tremor
in the hacking. It was a loaded down van,
a timer going off, a disconnected phone.
It was everything, the bull and the whip.
It was everyone registered in this
passive army against him. It was me,
pulling my weight. It was me, distracting.

Up Here With the Ground Below

I am sleepy. I'm the narcoleptic lover
snoring into your shoulder. I'm what's coming
back, what welcomes sorrow, the locked gate
that keeps you from running away. The petals
catch the light like metal. All that is
reflected there smiling in the sun,
this taking off, this breath I'm catching.
Up here with the ground below I am dreaming.
I am warming to the touch. I am left behind,
sealed in all my wings. The great flapper
in the sky rattles her beads and winds the
phonograph of her shame and naming.
You are Persephone returned. You are
to lead me out of the cave. All the coming back
and the weight of conviction, an underground forest.

Guitar Strings

I didn't need to know what
you used to whet me, what gauge
silk and sinew and slay
to woo me. I didn't need to know
how far to the sill of your strumming
me up to the saddle, stitching
my fluff back to the bridle.
I didn't need to know
how you found them
in an obscure music store
peddling 5-string banjos
exhibiting heart and a lyre
and a cure — mallets
for what you need to beat out.
Sing out. Sailing. Zing.
Stringing guts and clash,
wallets and ash.

After Words

Many worlds are possible
but we're stuck in just this
one. Everywhere I am you are
too, a click behind you, a page
away. Away from you I'm a bent
cable, a loose wire, a chunk
of solder — wrong place, wrong time, wrong
word. *Exceptional lenses into a future*
advertise in the socket of their square;
the few and the many lives written there,
a blaring, a jangle for spare change:
the storefront Santa, the baked clay
in Hayward, the misspelling Jones in his
covey of coterie, me in my unused
lingerie. The slip is just there for the rub,
my infatuation and an ink that wears off
in the handling. Your slips of tongue
in the swearing-in, the swearing. Those eyes
I am wearing to bed (by all accounts
on account of you)
while all around — an explosion
of worth, of asking. My hand in mine.

Home to You

Traveling to you I am home.
I am a vast continent unto myself.
Your return. My exile here.
Traveling to you I am one.
One sojourn's all it took,
a venture across enemy lines
(every lynch-tree, every
acre of green.) I admire
your sensuous thigh, battle
eaten, the shrapnel penetrating
still what still beats under that pelt.
Traveling to you I am there.
Sure in my shoes. Barefoot
in your warren of boxes.
I am returning to what you embrace.
I am nuzzling your arm again as if
I never left. I was going back
to where I began, an exile
of the heart.

A Bit of Grace

Cuarto

"Into the first world."
—T. S. Eliot

Crystal Clear Or Gibberish

for Stephen

After I said, "I love you,"
you could have hammered me over
the head with the silence. The flaccid
heart, the only music in our sphere.
I held you there, suspended in suspense
before rolling off and curling into a sticky
snail. It was all the blossoms falling
off the cherry tree in the hail, a slumber
of vultures circling my apartment,
a single red fox in my left-over garden
in a place someone is leaving; it was
all the kittens in the litter dying at once.

Shelling the Pecans

for Alfred Arteaga

I knew what a woman's hand could do:
shred the husk into threads, weave lips
together at the seam. Rock to hard body,
empire to thrust into knave — the native
touch tocando música up the spine
of the violin, some song of silk and gut.
I knew race was a matter of degree,
that inch in the face, that notice
of dismissal. How to work all day
at a posture, at a stance, at attention
paying attention to none but the awl.

I put my hole into you, this notch
between the breasts, this discovery
and treason. Hembra a macho. Fixed.
O defined in the still shell of history,
a destiny written in the charts and lost. Lost
in the unnoticed memories of you, a flicker
of change, some small scrimp
of light. Tu luz. Ahí allá — a la ala
and the scoop. Your águila eyes sweeping
up the dawn's desire. This night. I remember

shelling the pecans. Nothing but a bucket.
No ride exceptional. Nothing but a dream
to entertain us. I dreamed this moment —
all the sweet meats in a risen weight going
higher to the rim. The price and the pricing.
I could eat what I missed or messed. Outside,
the birds bending to it on a summer day.

The great age of my grandmother's banded
hand weighing me down. The paper
of tutelage blasting me away

at that age. Now, I still remember
how to shuck, how to fetch it, how to
step it. Stepping up to you, I ask.
The point enters the ventricle without
shattering the meat. How a woman
on a good day can rip out the heart
whole.

For ...

I saw the ocean
in your eyes, touched
your heart, once,
a subtle lapping
under the fingers.

A soft evaporation
left its mark
and something burrowed
in the fleshy sand;
your harvest, a thing

of the past. What
is past refuses
to stay under its
underlines — the headlines
under your brow, the mad

believing. I walk the tidelines,
the furrows, the sorrows,
the bright bridges into
tomorrow. The digging
continues, a gouging

under sentences. If I
were this belief I would
flourish, fly over crag
stone and reef. I wouldn't
stay here, fast and locked

in this absence of you.
All the possibilities become
you: a flinch in time,
an unreeling. The spools
of our separate lives run

out on their own. The great
fish of the heart, spawning
under its river, tight-fisted
as shark, The greening love
of sea — left — unbelieved.

Blood Moon, 7:45

for John

For a brief moment in time
the eye of the moon gazed
down upon my past loves, past
heart-wonders, upon you, my past lover.
For a while before it became
a sliver of a skiff, you and I,
the Owl and the Pussycat, were in love
once more inside a silver boat sailing
on the sea of sky — and almost disappeared
or dipped behind a star. Our lovespittle
descending down, our salivation,
our salvation of the moment
before the amorous fuzz that became
us was no more. No matter
what science finds us here (there),
two love-sucked suckers in a field
of budding roses turning the great dial
and straining against the pawl. All
that time I thought I knew you,
fed you a moment of me. Every cliche
tucked neatly in place, snug as
the diamond you placed upon my hand,
our pawnshop find, our brilliant
glass act. We were a sensuous lot,
a cipher coming home, our signals
strong as the waves crashing upon our shore.
Do you evermore? I hope so. There
where the mist envelopes, just over
that ridge where the light, now a nail
without a finger, points. For a moment

we were a phenomenon I will remember
to the grave. Or until fire becomes me
and I peer out upon a lucid bay
again. Under this blood moon drawing
our animal souls from home, I am
once again with you, gazing into
that part of myself who sits here
still. That heart that still loves
you — before the season passes,
before this changeling light disappears
into a blood mush and reappears,
changed. Same moon. Same face.
Same love, but shadowed and reinvented.
Soon to be, again, mundane
as that moon now refracting the sun's dial.
And I'm left here, dialing alone,
and wondering of you, your total
eclipse from me. And, move on.

The Ephemera of the Durable

for Michael Rossman

How much I would love a man
who knows the names of things — of feldspar
daggers and obsidian rain, able to distinguish
bone from fossilized coral, limestone from
cobble, who can count his own destiny
from the number of stars present
at his birth, the sum of the precise amount
of seconds each lived at that exact moment
of now when we kiss for the first
mixing of vital fluids — a vital man like that.

How much I would love a boy
who blew life back into a dissected roadkill
squirrel with a straw — who tried to nurse a puppy
born without a mouth or eyes to see him do it, who
then bashed in its head when he could do nothing more
than feed its drowning hole, his young tears watering
the flowers of his old man's soul-search, a searching
boy grazing the gifts of Mt. Talmapais on his own,
ever mining the veins of a humorous universe
of mirth, a boy in a man — a vital man, like that.

How much I would love an old man
and his hammer—the leathery rock
hound under a volcano sun, a man in a hat
with a boy's tanned chest and a forest
of sexual wisdom, his hardness"
"7.5 versus 7 for normal quartz", a man
it would take a whole lifetime to meet, all

my millions of molecules moving through the slate
to reach its like, aching to touch that balance
of play and dance and matrix — a vital man (like that).

How much I would love that old man
and want him to be my old man, to hear him
piping , the twinkle fast in his eye, a smiling man
unless discussing the follies of a fascist state,
a ripening man, a piper man I would follow
like a duck follows a dog, like the dumb earth
believes it follows an erratic Mercury, that impish
messenger, that winged passion; how much I would love
to see him singing under orchids again; how much
I would love to love that man—a vital man: like that.

California Gold Rush

for me

I went to Colorado
looking for love. I found
the hardest vein of shale
in the West — but none
as lasting as those lumps
of jade resting in the back
creek mouths, the polished
pebbles in the decisive
surf. I found a ragged trail
through to heart, but for the overgrown
shadows hugging the cliff, the blood red
sunsets on the Flatirons outside
my living room, the garnets of lady
bugs clustering into Berber rugs
of pilgrimage — I would still be there
if they had been enough — for us.
Alive, all of it, a moving mass
of prayer, a silent song they dance
to in the fall wind. I will miss
the love of the land, the love
of the migratory, all the tiny
souls caught in the horizon
of a sailor's dawn, the warning
in the gut in the silence of a single
lover. I went to Colorado
to find the love of my life,
for hiking in the woods of my want,
for ignoring the stupidity of the world
in the arms of another, for puzzling
my evenings away into the entire

photograph, for the picture postcards
formed by my days in the midst and mist
of these mountains. I loved. And I found
all these rocks of regret, all my broken
memories tossed out onto the road
overlooking a chasm we've yet to cross,
some expressway of the smarting
heart. I give it up. I bank on the stall
and glide into the future of my past.
Past the gulping rage that smacks
so many of my sucked up companions:
the clinking and the crash
of glass, of ice, breaking and breaking
up. I give it up. And come back here
to the hardest streets of culture
clashing into misery, where the songs
of my freedom replay still on the radio
of this chugging love. I keep on truckin'
like a river, a river I step into
again and again, the same river
twice.

After Heraclitus

for Alfred

You can step in the same river
twice. Be there in the flow
of sweet water, reason raining on
the face of it. All of it. El mismo
destino. Breaking away from it:
swirling picks of ice, sex foam,
fins. The fist of it in the pit,
a pock of light, surrendering.

Gather up the window of your mirada.
Hold it there, in the flame of cold
renewal. An arc of blessing, the stunned
fish fresh from the grab. Here
in the sudden treasure, a glimpse
of what huddles in the heart of the word,
the winding regouging, the recompense
of cliff rock, the breaking; this
breakwater of you stopping the flood,
the force of the drop that cracks the other
open. Open. All penumbra and flush.
All windswept and rush. All sweet
taste and gush. Again.

Post-Impression: I

for Webb

I want to be the couple
in a starry starry night,
an old fishwife, blood
on her skirt, her husband
under a hat. I want to be
luminous, a single blot
of paint, the canvas of your
eye, a duo on shallow wallow.
I want the arc of moon
in the vacant road, a sudden swath
of carnelian paradise, the layering
of dark upon dusk upon our arrival
of the final departure. I want
the shawl of a couple, nearly
unseen, just serene shadowing.
Let me be in the shining, in the light
of something impasto: memory
into sludge, into the distance
beginning.

Wild Ginger

for Honolulu

We'll last as long
as this ginger blossom,
the fragile white and not
the everlasting red, her kissing
cousin. Lavender orchid sings
to the orange crested shabby
bird who looks in through
the window. His mate sunning
her body on the splintered rail.
What blessing, these small
remembrances, worships at the nest,
wee flickers of meat or seed.
I wasn't born to wonder
at the fall or the fall
of all of it. But, wonder
what will fall of it, what chaff
fly off, what express ticket,
what impetuous nerve to fray
or remain. What, yes, what
will remain of it? The crazy waft
of ginger? A rare perfume in a certain
place? My arm about your neck?
Autumn in the still factory
where human error and willing
practice will prevail: a solemn
bow, a girlish twirl, a ripened
aging into sweet. We sweat
the sweet fragrance of spring
gone ahead on to summer.
Here, above the driest part

of the island that we are unto
ourselves. Some bird call,
animal tick, a flicker of leg,
a flick of tail could be
a warning. I'll take this fruit
as it ripens, stop to smell
the flower of our past, our loves
and failings and learn to love
this ancient jungle, this tumbling
in the grit and grunt. We'll last
as long as ginger blooms in the dish
or a bird in hand or the everlasting
'cense.

Nothing Lasts

for my dad, for Alfred

Only the land lasts, not you.
Only your steps upon it, the cut
glass of memory and your smile within
it survives. Only the land lasts; simple rock
and the dumb scape of lusting lack,
the rack and pinion of flight and fall.
Autumn doesn't last. Not spring
with all its fine tithings. Not the shine
of those young girls' hair, not the waists
of women, not the fading fire. Not you
and the way we were. Only the land
lasts, and the ridges of waiting wearing
out the pursed lips of furrowed ranges,
and not the cold within their lair. Only
the stunned shale, the red-faced cliffs,
the heights where someone sometime ascended
and stood, and loved, the land layering there
laid out in its full affair, the glinting
mica and dream of hard brooding diamonds,
all the hidden glory, the unseen flake
of gold and petrified burl. Not this
hand stroking life into an empty palm,
the smooth skin of summer, the sudden
skim of a wayward glance. Nothing of you
or the lonelier retreat of other
killer mammals and their heat.
Nothing lasts but the land, not the water
or the tearing, not the creeks and the clearings,

not the withered heart nor the soiled clothing
of social graces, nor the mouthy flaring
of wondered disgrace. Nothing lasts of this house,
not the boards nor the worms nor the birds. Not
the words I use to slow it down and make it stick.
Nothing lasts like the red clouds on the day
of your passing, the wicked gassing
or the olvido of oblivion. Nothing lasts
but this sand drained of you, your sea;
this chiseled frown in the chipped flint,
this skirting of canyon, this flaw and filing,
this grinding down but lasting, the silk touch
in a handhold, in the holding out for the summit.
Nothing but the wounding in the craters,
the uplift and the gurgling lava; all the ways
we read a stone's hieroglyphics, the ore's heavy lead.
Were we to discover, we would uncover a myth,
the stories we tell to renew the pact
with this earth. This, love. Nothing lasts
but the land and our love
of it.

Pfeiffer Beach

Lavender clings to the cliff.
I left this long ago. Yellow
lupine slings her slipper, small moss
hands shiver in the stilled wind. Hello
past. Goodbye fading future into
now. The eternity of the sea waves
her saludos. Sometimes something turns
and the bit pawl slips, the ratchet sawing
away at my face slows for an instant
and I see. Summer sludges up the hill
as the sun burns through until
frost. And here I am. Not hurrying.
Breathing in the medicine breath of eucalyptus
as the hillsides burst into the many erections
of buckeye, their flagrant white
penises trumping the bees. We called them
Coyote Trees, Trickster Bushes, always changing
shape. The shape-shifters along this path I'm on
beckon. The whole world beckons. And I'm traveling
on.

Monterey

Every ending finds its own
beginning, the broken beetle curled
into its hovel, the leaves and leavings
of the world gone crisp. All of it

in a loop of sense, the still burning,
and its ash. The seed in me
bares wings, nubbins to the last.
I take the last oranges on the wiry stem,

the then and now expurgated in its scent.
And remember you, my face, my mirror,
my tunneling in the remembrance — a sprig
of bouganvillea, vibrant and calling

the memory home: a memory of home,
or some kind of smoke. A haze
over days, and, the dissipation.
I believe that the butterfly finds

its lost scale, all the scuffled dust
that keeps it aloft. I believe that what
sleeps in its hollowed den wakens
and feeds, and needs the nuzzlings

it finds there. I believe that the sea
in its spiral cage looks out the cephalopod's
wake. All of spring in its burgeoning fate
repeats. And I am. Repeating. I am.

And I'm not. And I wait.

A Bit of Grace

Quinto

"My Soul has grown deep like the river."
—Langston Hughes

Fear of Death

Marta had a fear of death, she wouldn't
sleep for the child still caught in her throat,
the insomniac who counted stars and crumbs
of cake. She couldn't let go. It followed
her to school. It drank from her glass
of milk in the morning. It soiled her
shoes. Marta had a fear of falling
asleep and never waking up, of discovering
that the migra of the waking world had just asked
for her papers and that she'd be hauled into
the cell of the earth for processing. Marta
had a fear of certain things: the sharp end
of the knife, the hissing gas. But mostly
of sleep and pain, that final composition
of the heart: "*I I I will will will not
not not fear fear fear my my my
life.*"

A Chicano Poem

for Librotraficante

They tried to take our words,
Steal away our hearts under
Their imaginary shawls, their laws,
Their libros, their *Libranos Señor.*
No more. They tried to take
Away our Spirit in the rock, the Mountain,
The Living Waters. They tried to steal
Our languages, our grandmothers' pacts,
Our magma cartas for their own serfs.
They razed the land and raised a Constitution,
Declared others 3/5ths a human being,
Snapped shackles, cut off a foot,
Raped our grandmothers into near mute
Oblivion. They burned the sacred codices
And the molten goddesses rose anew
In their flames. They tried to silence a
Nation, tried to send The People back
To the Four Corners of the world. They drew
A line in the sand and dared us to cross it,
Tried to peel off our skins, Xipe Totec
Screaming through our indigenous consciousness.
They tried to brand "America" into our unread
Flesh, the skull and crossbones flying at
Half-mast. They tried to put their eggs in
Our baskets, tried to weave the Native
Out of us with their drink and drugs, tried to
Switch their mammy-raised offspring, beaded and
Unshaven, as the colorless pea under our mattresses
In a cultural bait and switch, hook and bait.
They tried to take our words,
Give us the Spanish translation for

"Pain," serve us the host of fallow fields on a
China plate, stripped us of the germ and seed,
Fed us in a steady diet of disease and famine.
Where is the word for tomorrow to the dead?
When is our kingdom come? They claim our
Reclamations; our reparations, a thing of our
Imaginations. I discover this truth
To be self-evident: In the beginning
We were here.
I declare us here today
And speaking.

False Eyelashes

You were ten-up but we cut you
some slack. Made up the pact
by pulling out. You seeded
out of high school, succeeded
out on sex; redressed and
second guessed, you ceded
out on semblance, lanced
the blister of your heart, the
sap ran dry and slow as a
losing math test, oozing
down the avenues; you,
sequestered in satin,
a cat in the sink, a
secret, the reword of you
in a vision of glue.

Sunshine Knife Blades

Fifteen years old in five year old jeans,
my shepherd pup, my traveling rainbow,
my loyal thumb
bulging with desire. My road
rutted and rutting, my dead ahead
sorrow. My moccasined feet
rolling in small kisses of bruising,
a cartography of touch
languishing over the tan.

He put his necklace of
anger safe at my throat.
My ivory recorder, a still
white bird in my lap. An avenue
of alcoholic vapor filled the fear.
In those days our pass to pass
was our smile. Innocence
was a gumball treasure
and all our pockets were picked.

Whetted, whelped, well
on our way out — we hemmed
up the fortune of our flounce
and folded into ourselves,
jack-knifed on the dare — and glinting.

First Impression: Gossip

All the valley rang out, the tardy bell
of the seasons clanging through the buzz
of bees. The saturated heart, sticky
with sweet. The field, the field, a golden
hue, a hum, a hand. I shot her
a glance. Her starched soul shimmered
in the heat. Her baked hands, never idle,
tending, tending to touch. All the bay
was a ring of gold fading into rainbow.
The carriage of the sun armoring its horses.
Had I wanted to, I might have done so,
carried the sword through the stone,
extended my light, shut off the stares
of the knaves. My classmates shining
there, pent up in pants and plastic
shoes. My starched white dress, my
petticoat itching; my ten cent token
burning a hole to a destination:
some kind of charted landscape,
some unchartered territory becoming
only a number. And I find it. Recovery.

My Daddy's Car

I never saw my father drive. I saw my
father's clever Zoot Suit, the crease
in his pants, the duck tail soup
of his permanent wave. I never saw
a key in his hand, the metal jangling,
heard him swear at the error of others:
the deadly choices, the limits of the lanes
of terror. My father lived through dooms
of love, a poet sang it, e e singing
the singing love of his father. I never heard
the swerve, the stunned slow and the brake.
My father walked through fields of mustard,
toting what he willed. My father's slight
form conforming to the wilded hay.
I never saw my father drive. My father,
impeccable in his smell. The grinning
earth of his laugh, that blossoming.
His whitening sound, his worked for
musculature — his steady holding
of the hundred pound weight. The line
presses on like a heart, a continual
reel in the baking. I pull it in,
that remedy for bluing, that tempering
for the rusted stain. But not the soft
ball field of indecision. Not an umpire
within site. Just me and the lingering
flapping. This memory that drives.

Quadruple Peach

Chones's lowrider was the baddest
around, all breathing on its haunches
like a bucking ass. Chone polished
the glass, licked the chrome when no
one was watching and only gassed up
at the station where his Tío Chucho
worked. Chone wiped the whole ride
down with his chones. That's how
he got the name. That, and as Betita
said, "He was kind of an ass."

He poured his soul into the car.
All the money he got his hands
on he gave to that metal. His ruca
watched television in the dark dusk,
the twinkling lights of passing sedans
making shadow plays on her tired face.

Chone hit the big time, in his quadruple
peach. But he never got the pit.

Cheese

Man, Chucho was cheesy
when he was in love.
He was like poked full of holes,
with a cute cartoon mouse
peeking out of them. Chucho's
eyes were puffy with love, a pair
of twin brown marshmallows
held too long to the fire.
Chucho was all in love.
It made his pants fall down
because he wouldn't eat anything
but caldo. He spent all his
time in the mirror or kissing
his pillow in secret, the milk
of his soul pooling out
in a thick slab of himself
in love con La Ella.

A Hard Drive

Esa chica was hard to drive, Reyes spoke,
mumbling into his mug. She wouldn't lay
4 on the floor, wouldn't squeal on a dime
or do donuts in the parking lot. "Maybe it's time
to trade her in," he repeated. "Get at least
something for my money." Yes, this little
chica's always been the one to walk — late
at night between the 7-11 and the stars,
she'd come to, some somnambulist gymnast
in the night when the shift came off in his
hand, and there she was — all chrome
and shine and oiled. *Pero esa chica was
hard to drive.* She wouldn't do it all.
She balked on the turn and wouldn't
speed up on the entry way. One free
way over nine, a sunny equation on her
face. You could do with her as you
will, but her will was filled up, and was
making her go.

The 4-Barrel Carburetor On a '72 Chevy Camaro

He could make love like a 4-barrel
carburetor on a '72 Chevy
Camaro. Man, he could go. Pumping up
the pistons, discharging with a growl.
He wasn't all that to look at, mostly gleaming
chrome and wire. Slick in the upholstery
and revved. He was a 2-bucket seat
palace, a chariot of wiles. He was
coming back. He was a place off the map.
He was coming home and he was moving.
He was a reserved parking space, a handicapped
spot on the heart. He was a ticket
waiting to be written, a stop-on-a-
dime promise of forgiveness. He could
pick up in the alley, carry away on the charm
of his engine. All the draft on a knife
point of design and desire, his get up
and go: his knack.

Hips Hitting the Floor

She was a mariposa and the sweet
vines of men on the sidewalk were her
bounty. She wore the shackles of mascara
under a thick veil of a Chanel knock-off. She let her
hands talk, the rhythm of her walk, a serenata
to nada and a way of letting go. "Come
with me," she would call out to the boys.
And one by one the constitution of
America would fall. All of them, amendments
vetoed in the spring, were kicked off
the table as it was, hips hitting the floor;
flung glasses of rage between the sudden kiss
and miss.

Child Prostitution

I notice banana leaves airing
their sorrows in the shadows.
I notice the path, the stones and their treacherous
wiles, the uneven distribution in the walk.
I notice girls, waving the brown
fronds in a wind of their own making,
the burden of their breasts, the shallow
waist, the foto of their days, never
developed. I shake the empty tree,
green nubbins, aborted. The heavy juices,
tangled and teased. I saw a barrio
there. A life full of promise. A rare flight,
the willful might of their choices.
Every day was a week and a half;
the tight seas within them, seething;
the sensuous allies in their redistribution.
I saw the lines of chalk before they were drawn,
the long drawn-out war of their making.
I saw the most beautiful apples tear
from the tree, the mush-bellied falling,
the know-nothing heart would now
grin it or bear. I saw temperance
in their hands, but could not find them.
As I saw the chipped concrete of the barrio
there. The tight vaginas of enchantment
in the empty stream. What will translate
this into a country? an art? the yellow
peel? What moment would I move?
What will deliver? What won't say?
What will go? *"I saw a barrio there.*
Every day was a week and a half."

Social Responsibility (Community)

Before this light, the shadow in the hair.
Before this circle, a stick in the dirt.
Before this breath, a hundred wings, unfurling.
Before this flag, a hundred thousand hands,
and they are hurting. All the world, an emblem,
entire strands of genes in the soup and
spelling our names. Another shot in the
dark corner. Another word stuck in the slot.
After this shadow, another strand of night.
After this crevice, another clod coming unstuck.
After this feather, a thousand lungs giving up.
After this responsibility, an entire community
getting lost. All the world is final
in your loving way. All the words
come to and gather at the river. All
the nests become this bird, this hand,
this right.

The End of Her Life

was a broken line, unsigned, forever.
It was a turned off searchlight
from an empty parking lot, was a lake
at the end of the road, the bridge burned
out, the barricade that wouldn't hold.

The end of her life was an empty notebook,
was a blank receipt, a return, an exchange.
The end of her life was the black muck from the bottom,
was the last string to let out the kite,
was the last frijól to scrape from the pot.

The end of her life was a single stop
sign that everyone ran through, a toll
bridge without anyone in the booth
to collect her change, was a whistling
kettle — no one left in the house to release
her from the flame.

The end of her was the last note
in the sonata, the failing breath, the holding in
was the shut book, the turned off light in a room
full of daylight. Who would notice her passing?
who didn't love her?

Hologram Roses

for Mom

You were a shattered mirror,
disaster in the state
of disrepair — the kitchen sink,
languorous with buzzings
and the swift shadows
on the plastic counters.

Heaven didn't reward you.
Fate saw it through.
Your thinking of a future
banned at the gate,
the sensuous censors
of a young girl's treason.

You loved like that, lived
a paper trail of debt and dues,
discovered a continent
of flay and flaw. And leapt.
Into your past, heart-first;
a trailing meteor, a lit ember,
a hologram rose.

Fire Blackens the Broken Rib

for Orlando Ramírez and Adrian Rocha

In a circle of silence we nested.
Around a cement ring we danced. Bob Marley,
wailing the summer down, sang of
porridge, "and it was love-wood burning
through the night." In those years
of pay and earn, we pooled our seeds
and pulled up heads of pungent bulbs.
The boards we gleaned from busted homes
wormed with embers. One cracked
the cement sewer pipe into grill
and together, we, poets, put our
flesh to the test; watching fire
blacken the broken rib.

The City

It's fall in The City and I've fallen
into the city of my birth, City of
Mirth. The stubborn sun, a willful
wind, and this, the sun splats on the
streets, we, writers.
I've returned. It was never really
home so I can go home again. I've come
to the base of this hill, the corner of
living and working, and working at living —
and it's still.

I Always Wanted to Be Neruda

I always wanted to be
Neruda, fine-boned
and a lyre. It seems so
close and too far. Too
near the sea or somewhere
else distant as a bird's
calling, a toad croaking
unto sorrow (silly mucker
in the wait and wade), a wake
in the throat, all the chorus
married off or passed
on, on to the river, the
river that has never looked
so precious, all pewter
polish, hand-hewn heart
wood. Would I a willow
and a willow's charm I'd
rend you, try and trial, but
fishing until death, that hag's
head looming on the mid-way horizon
barren as an absent mother.
Do I do you this rest?
Do I bear?

I quest.
I quest.
I quest

and risk sounding stupid
as the elkhorn's holler,
some original sincerity

rising in the hollow,
sounds. Rising, in a musky
twist of fate, a bed. A bud.
I always wanted to be
Neruda, sing of the love
in an oaken barrel, in the barrel
of an anger situated after
birth, some mother of cloud
bank pressing its finger in
at the Gulf. Is it windy enough?
Were I with you enough
I'd be stripped to the looted
shelves, my entropy
holding fast, gripping as a
ring, a fitted suit, the fitting suit
and suite of a full house
singing — the wry wine
of Neruda in his shell
of a house, on his shell
of a coral island ridden
with shells and coral death
masks. To live amid
the litter, to love among
the drawl and coo. You, too,
a galaxy of indecision,
some Perseidean torrent
in a time. I always wanted
to be Neruda. Sing of love
and war. Wear my sombrero.
Back to the biting cacti. To be
scorpion to the cholla, the
tarantula nesting in the Century
juice in the stick and
the comfort, an ambassador
to the country of a loving name,

any pass, a port of call,
a rustling of this corazón
espinado. Listening.
A hummingbird's heart to the 9th
dimension, a poet of hope
and resistance, pride of sunflower
or the surprise of soft flesh
in the artichoke's heart. How
many hearts does it take
to make a core? Name this
and you have a poem. Live
this and you have a life. Love
this and you have a heart,
the heart of a poet, so many
times over — the bullets in the
gun, all the bills in the wallet
of war — an intervention but
no Pablo which never was
his real name. For real. A poet.
To have the ballot but not the poem. . .
To have the poet but not the home. . .

I never will be
Pablo Neruda.
But a poet, a woman's
bird chinking the links
of the cage, her revolving
loves winding down, ridden
unto river — winning the war
but never the song, the love,
the poem.

The Latin Girl Speaks of Rivers

When I wrote about the serpentine
river I was really writing about
a rape. When I wrote about the moon
over an oak tree I was writing about
a preteen pregnancy. When I wrote
about the crystalline sea I was writing
all the horror around me into intricate
filigree. I was writing my heart out. I was
writing myself back in. When I wrote about heart
I imagined a muscle of infinite distance,
of the brave little choo-choo times ten. I
was dreaming of a heart-shaped boat, an extension
of my past, my trapped beginnings.
When I wrote of a river it was one
I could get myself into twice. It was
wide as an Anglo-dammed Nile, long
as the Negro Mississippi. I wanted
to wrench myself a new closure. I wanted
the tourniquet and the cannon. I wanted
the white water to sail me to a place
where the journey never ends — instead
of the endless fluid nights. I wanted the fissures
to heal of their own magma. I wanted
something of the banks to make clay,
to make me a setting at someone's bountiful
table. I wanted real silver on the plaits
of that liquid path. I wanted its icy skin
to burn against mine, to cleave with each lap,
and run, like the fallen log I was. I wanted
the box of my childhood to open. I wrote

longing in some minor key about a crystalline river, about the telling moon, about a single leaf that could carry me home, about the knowing sea, about me.

About the Author

A fifth generation Californian of Californio and Native American (Chumash) heritage, Lorna Dee Cervantes was a pivotal figure throughout the Chicano literary movement. She began publishing the literary journal *Mango* in 1976. Her small press of the same name was widely admired for its creative designs and for the important voices it introduced, including Sandra Cisneros, Gary Soto, Luís Omar Salinas, and Alberto Ríos.

Her poetry has appeared in hundreds of anthologies and literary magazines, and she has been featured in *Bloomsbury Review* and *World Literature Today*. Cervantes' first book, *Emplumada* (University of Pittsburgh, 1981), received the American Book Award. Her second collection, *From the Cables of Genocide: Poems on Love and Hunger* (Arte Público, 1991) was awarded the Paterson Poetry Prize, the poetry prize of the Institute of Latin American Writers, and the Latino Literature Award. After a long silence, Cervantes published *DRIVE: The First Quartet* (Wings Press, 2006), a 300-page, five-volumes-in-one collection which won the International Latino Book Award. She has received two National Endowment for the Arts poetry fellowships and the prestigious Lila Wallace Readers Digest Writer's Award. She has twice been honored with a Pushcart Prize, including one for the poem "Shelling the Pecans," included in this volume.

After completing her doctoral work in History of Consciousness at UCSC, Cervantes was an associate professor of English for nineteen years and Director of Creative Writing at the University of Colorado in Boulder until she returned to her birthplace, San Francisco.

Acknowledgments

A "Shelling the Pecans" was originally published in *OCHO*, #6, 2006. Poem later won a Pushcart Prize and appeared in *Pushcart Prize XXXII: Best of the Small Presses*, 2008. It was included in *Best of MiPoesias*, 2012 and in *The MiPoesias iPad Companion*, 2012.

"Polygamy," "Slaughterhouse," "Language," "Tension In The Body" and "Strength" first appeared in *MiPoesias*, 2012.

"Post-Impression: 1" first appeared in *ElevenEleven*, #14, January, 2013.

"A Chicano Poem" and "Wet Feet" first appeared in *Huizache*, Fall, 2012.

"Burial" first appeared in *Harbinger Asylum*, Issue #3, 2011 and was included in *From One Sphere to Another: Best of Harbinger Asylum*, 2010-2012. February, 2013.

"Resurrection," "Blind Desert Snakes" and "Thunderheads" [as "(Clouds) Thunderheads"] appeared in *The Mas Tequila Review*, Issue Issue #5. Summer, 2012.

"Crystal Clear Or Gibberish" was published in *Ciento: 100 100-Word Love Poems* (Wings Press, 2011) in another version under the title, "Possibilities — In 100 Words."

"The Latin Girl Speaks Of Rivers" first appeared in *Stunned Into Being: Essays On The Poetry of Lorna Dee Cervantes*, Wings Press, 2011.

"I Always Wanted To Be Neruda," "Homegrown," "Sunshine Knife Blades," "First Impression: Gossip," "My Daddy's Car" [as "(Laundry, Washing) Or The Softball Field, My Daddy's Car"], "Fear of Death," Indigena," "A Hard Drive," "Hips Hitting The Floor," "Social Responsibility (Community)," "Child Prostitution," "Hometown," "Ver," "Blind Desert Snakes," "Night Travelers," "Thunderheads" [as "(Clouds) Thunderheads"], "The End of Her Life," "Pfeiffer Beach," "Monterey" and "The City" were first published in a special limited edition, *BIRD AVE y New Mission Poems* (MANGO Publications, 2008) for the Chicana/Latina Foundation.

"Burn Ward," "Crystal Clear Or Gibberish," "People Talking In Their Sleep," "Guitar Strings," "Love," "Yes," "Alas," "Promise," "Permanence," "Doppleganger," "Stress and Distress," "Up There With The Ground Below," "Wet Feet," "Allure," "Language," "After Words," "Shelling The Pecans," "For...," "Blood Moon: 7:45" [as "Blood Moon"], "California Gold Rush," "After Heraclitus" and "Nothing Lasts" appeared in a limited edition, *100 Word Love Poems & A Bit of Grace* (MANGO Pulications, 2008.)

Most of these poems appeared in draft form on Lorna Dee Cervantes's blog, LornaDice at lornadice.blogspot.com.

The author thanks "NaPoWriMo," National Poetry Writing Month, and all the poets participating by writing a poem a day in April. All poems in the first section of *Sueño*, "Thirty-Something of the Cruelest" were selected from poems written in April for NaPoWriMo, 2006-12.

The author would like to lovingly acknowledge her first teacher, Virginia de Araujo at her London Meadow Writers Workshop every Thursday night, 1973-78: Nothing is possible without your voice. Now gone, you still make it possible. Finally, the author wishes to thank her multi-talented publisher, Bryce Milligan, once again: "Patience is a virtue."

Wings Press was founded in 1975 by Joanie Whitebird and Joseph F. Lomax, both deceased, as "an informal association of artists and cultural mythologists dedicated to the preservation of the literature of the nation of Texas." Publisher, editor, and designer since 1995, Bryce Milligan has carried on and expanded that mission to include the finest in American writing—meaning *all* of the Americas, without commercial considerations clouding the choice to publish or not to publish.

Wings Press produces multicultural books, chapbooks, ebooks, and broadsides that, we hope, enlighten the human spirit and enliven the mind. Every person ever associated with Wings has been or is a writer. We believe that writing is a transformational art form capable of changing the world, primarily by allowing us to glimpse something of each other's souls. Good writing is innovative, insightful, and interesting. But most of all it is honest.

Likewise, Wings Press is committed to treating the planet itself as a partner. Thus the press uses as much recycled material as possible, from the paper on which the books are printed to the boxes in which they are shipped.

As Robert Dana wrote in *Against the Grain*, "Small press publishing is personal publishing. In essence, it's a matter of personal vision, personal taste and courage, and personal friendships." Welcome to our world.

Colophon

This first edition of *Sueño*, by Lorna Dee
Cervantes, has been printed on 55 pound
Edwards Brothers Natural Paper containing a
percentage of recycled fiber. Titles have been
set in Cochin type, the text in Adobe Caslon
type. All Wings Press books are designed and
produced by Bryce Milligan.

On-line catalogue and ordering:
www.wingspress.com

Wings Press titles are distributed
to the trade by the
Independent Publishers Group
www.ipgbook.com
and in Europe by
www.gazellebookservices.co.uk

Also available as an ebook.